DEC - - 2014

THE LIFE CYCLE OF A
Chicken

By Colleen Sexton

BELLWETHER MEDIA · MINNEAPOLIS, MN

Note to Librarians, Teachers, and Parents:

Blastoff! Readers are carefully developed by literacy experts and combine standards-based content with developmentally appropriate text.

Level 1 provides the most support through repetition of high-frequency words, light text, predictable sentence patterns, and strong visual support.

Level 2 offers early readers a bit more challenge through varied simple sentences, increased text load, and less repetition of high-frequency words.

Level 3 advances early-fluent readers toward fluency through increased text and concept load, less reliance on visuals, longer sentences, and more literary language.

Level 4 builds reading stamina by providing more text per page, increased use of punctuation, greater variation in sentence patterns, and increasingly challenging vocabulary.

Level 5 encourages children to move from "learning to read" to "reading to learn" by providing even more text, varied writing styles, and less familiar topics.

Whichever book is right for your reader, Blastoff! Readers are the perfect books to build confidence and encourage a love of reading that will last a lifetime!

This edition first published in 2011 by Bellwether Media, Inc.

No part of this publication may be reproduced in whole or in part without written permission of the publisher. For information regarding permission, write to Bellwether Media, Inc., Attention: Permissions Department, 5357 Penn Avenue South, Minneapolis, MN 55419.

Library of Congress Cataloging-in-Publication Data
Sexton, Colleen A., 1967–
 The life cycle of a chicken / by Colleen Sexton.
   p. cm. – (Blastoff! readers. Life cycles)
 Summary: "Developed by literacy experts for students in grades kindergarten through three, this book follows chickens as they transform from eggs to adults. Through leveled text and related images, young readers will watch these creatures grow through every stage of life"–Provided by publisher.
 Includes bibliographical references and index.
 ISBN 978-1-60014-450-9 (hardcover : alk. paper)
 1. Chickens–Life cycles–Juvenile literature. I. Title.
 SF487.5.S49 2010
 636.5–dc22   2010000705

Printed in the United States of America, North Mankato, MN.
080110   1162

Contents

rooster

Chickens are birds. Most chickens are raised on farms for their eggs and meat.

Male chickens are roosters.
Female chickens are hens.

hen

Chickens come in many colors and sizes.
They have wings to fly short distances.
Feathers keep their bodies warm.

Chickens have skinny legs. Their feet have claws. Chickens have red **combs** on top of their heads. Red **wattles** hang below their beaks.

comb

wattle

claws

Chickens grow and change in stages.
The stages of a chicken's **life cycle** are
egg, chick, and adult.

egg

chick

adult

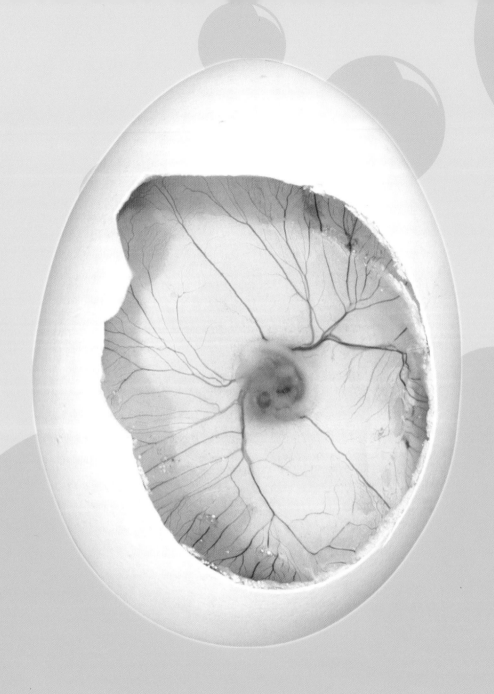

A chicken starts life as an egg. The egg's **yolk** and **white** are food for the chick.

The chick grows inside the egg for 21 days.
The mother hen sits on the egg to keep it warm.

The chick hatches. It uses its **egg tooth** to break out of the shell.

egg tooth

The chick's wet body dries quickly. It has fluffy feathers called **down**.

The chick can walk
and run a few hours
after it hatches.

The chick must be kept warm for the first week. The air where it lives should be about 95° Fahrenheit (35° Celsius).

The chick drinks water and eats a mix of grains, plants, meat, and **vitamins**.

The food helps the chick grow quickly.
The chick starts growing longer feathers.

At six weeks the chick starts to **roost**. It moves to a **perch** where it sleeps at night.

The chick is all grown up
when it is 20 weeks old.
She is a hen and is ready
to lay eggs.

A rooster **struts** around a hen and shows off his feathers. The rooster and the hen **mate**.

The hen prepares her nest. She sits in it and moves around to make it the right shape. She arranges and fluffs the **bedding**.

The hen lays an egg. The egg is the start of a new life cycle!

Glossary

bedding—the material used to make a nest; hay, wood shavings, and shredded paper are some types of bedding.

combs—fleshy parts on the heads of chickens that help keep them cool; roosters have larger combs than hens.

down—small, soft feathers

egg tooth—a sharp, hard point of skin on a chick's beak; the egg tooth falls off a few days after the chick hatches.

life cycle—the stages of life of an animal; a life cycle includes being born, growing up, having young, and dying.

mate—to join together to produce young

perch—a pole or rod that a chicken wraps its feet around

roost—to rest or sleep on a perch

struts—walks proudly

vitamins—substances found in food and nature that help animals grow and stay healthy

wattles—fleshy parts that hang below the beaks of chickens; wattles do not have a purpose.

white—the thick, clear liquid around the yolk of an egg; the egg white is food for a chick while it is growing inside an egg.

yolk—part of an egg that is food for an animal; the yolk is food for a chick while it is growing inside an egg.

To Learn More

AT THE LIBRARY

Gibbons, Gail. *Chicks and Chickens*. New York, N.Y.: Holiday House, 2003.

Green, Emily K. *Chickens*. Minneapolis, Minn.: Bellwether Media, 2007.

Ray, Hannah. *Chickens*. Laguna Hills, Calif.: QEB Publishing, 2006.

ON THE WEB

Learning more about life cycles is as easy as 1, 2, 3.

1. Go to www.factsurfer.com.

2. Enter "life cycles" into the search box.

3. Click the "Surf" button and you will see a list of related Web sites.

With factsurfer.com, finding more information is just a click away.

Index

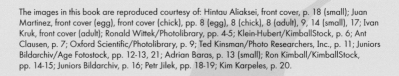

The images in this book are reproduced courtesy of: Hintau Aliaksei, front cover, p. 18 (small); Juan Martinez, front cover (egg), front cover (chick), pp. 8 (egg), 8 (chick), 8 (adult), 9, 14 (small), 17; Ivan Kruk, front cover (adult); Ronald Wittek/Photolibrary, pp. 4-5; Klein-Hubert/KimballStock, p. 6; Ant Clausen, p. 7; Oxford Scientific/Photolibrary, p. 9; Ted Kinsman/Photo Researchers, Inc., p. 11; Juniors Bildarchiv/Age Fotostock, pp. 12-13, 21; Adrian Baras, p. 13 (small); Ron Kimball/KimballStock, pp. 14-15; Juniors Bildarchiv, p. 16; Petr Jilek, pp. 18-19; Kim Karpeles, p. 20.